CONTENTS

INTRODUCTION

Chicken is our favourite meat these days. In Britain we eat more chicken meat in all sorts of ways than any other, and it's a trend that is growing. What's more we eat most of it at home. Of course there is a lot of chicken served in restaurants and even fast food shops, but we like to cook it and eat it at our own tables most of all.

There are a number of reasons for this; flavour and texture have a lot to do with it. Almost everyone likes the mild savoury taste and the firm yet tender toothsomeness of chicken. Then there is the health issue; low in fat and high in protein, chicken is the perfect ingredient in a society where red meat is steadily falling out of fashion. It is also easy to cook, at least the kind of chicken we get these days is. I sometimes regret the passing of the 'boiling' fowl, a bird that may have needed an hour or more's cooking, but had its reward in extra flavour. Today's birds come in a number of varieties, but they are all tender and quick to cook.

The varieties are worth remarking on. Without question the best value, and astonishingly good value it is too! are the standard chilled chickens. They come in a number of sizes and are a little more costly than frozen birds, but far better in flavour. Corn fed chickens with their notable golden skin are also widely available, as are other 'grain fed' versions. Some people find them better, but apart from the colour and the assurance that they have been fed on vegetable diets, they are produced in very similar intensive rearing techniques to their chilled cousins. Free range birds, whether from Britain or Europe have a slightly more spacious life than that, and a little exercise, which improves their texture as well as taste. Best of all, though rare and expensive, are organically produced chickens, which can be a revelation to eat. Lastly there are Poussin, small chickens bred that way, not killed young. They are raised on a quite humane basis with an outstanding flavour, and are very convenient when cooking for small numbers. There is also the difference it makes to be able to buy portions today, whether you want boneless thighs, or just breasts or even chicken mince, the convenience pack is available.

But perhaps most important of all is the versatility of chicken. As I hope you will find in this book, there are recipes of all sorts. Wonderful old fashioned (and new fashioned) roasts, exotic curries, quick stir-fries and gently cooked casseroles. There are delicate lunch dishes and light-weight salads, together with solid suppers and rib sticking bakes. I've used all the bits of the bird, from the elusive giblets through the exclusive supremes, to the stock from the bones. Starters and mains, soups and sauces are all here. The only thing that is missing is the Cock a doodle doo.

I do hope you will enjoy all the varied and delicious dishes that I have compiled from my favourite 'crafty' chicken recipe collection.

CHICKEN STOCK

Not only does this make a marvellous soup on its own, but it is the basis of so many chicken dishes. To make great chicken stock start with a chicken or as much of it as you can. A carcass, wing tips, giblets and even thoroughly washed feet can be used; but not the liver as it makes the stock go cloudy.

INGREDIENTS
1 chicken carcass (this can be lightly roasted in the oven for 30 minutes before using)

1 onion	2 peppercorns
Pinch of salt	2 pints water

For the bouquet garni:

2 bay leaves	2 sprigs thyme
Stalks of a bunch of parsley	Central stem of a head of celery

Put all the ingredients into a large saucepan, bring to the boil and simmer for 45 minutes to an hour. Strain into a large bowl.

Let the stock cool, then refrigerate. The fat floats to the top, solidifies after a few hours and lifts off effortlessly.

CANTONESE CHICKEN AND SWEETCORN SOUP

This is one of the most popular soups in Chinese restaurants – and one which children seem to like as much as grown-ups. Serves 4.

INGREDIENTS
1 medium onion, peeled and finely chopped
2.5 cm/1 in piece fresh root ginger, peeled and finely chopped
2 tbsp cooking oil
1 pinch five spice powder
900 ml/1½ pints chicken stock – fresh or stock cube
350 g/12 oz sweetcorn kernels, frozen or tinned
30 g/1 oz cornflour
1 chicken breast cut into very small dice
4 spring onions, trimmed and finely chopped

Heat the oil in a large pan and fry the onion and ginger gently for 3 minutes. Add the five spice powder, the stock and sweetcorn, bring to the boil, cover and simmer for 15 minutes.

Mix the cornflour to a paste with a little water and stir into the soup. Bring back to the boil and remove from the heat. Put two ladlefuls of the soup – about 225 ml/8 fl oz – into a food processor or liquidizer and whizz until smooth. Return to the pan, add the finely diced chicken, stir well and simmer for 5 minutes.

Garnish with finely chopped spring onions and serve in Chinese bowls – or the prettiest ones you have!

Cantonese Chicken & Sweetcorn Soup

CHICKEN BARLEY SOUP

A real warming farmhouse-style soup. It's very simple to make and, depending on what root vegetables are available, you can vary the ingredients. It's also one of those soups that benefits from being reheated the next day, though it may need a little more liquid, as the barley will absorb the juices. Serves 4.

INGREDIENTS
50 g/2 oz butter
225 g/8 oz each onion, leek, turnip and carrot, cut into 1 cm/½ in pieces
100 g/4 oz pearl barley
2 celery sticks, sliced
1 tsp salt
freshly ground black pepper
1.2 litres/2 pints chicken stock
100 g/4 oz parsley, chopped

Melt the butter in a deep saucepan, add the diced vegetables, pearl barley and celery. Season with the salt and pepper to taste and add the stock. Simmer for 40 minutes, until the vegetables are tender and the barley is swollen and cooked through (test a bit between your teeth to make sure).

To serve, put a spoonful of chopped parsley in each bowl and pour the soup over it to get a thorough mix and a bright green colour that sets off the more subtle earthy tones of the soup.

COCKIE LEEKIE SOUP

A Scottish soup of heartening flavour and some unusual ingredients. Have courage: the prunes are traditional and the tastes do go wonderfully together. Serve with hot oat bread. Serves 4.

INGREDIENTS
1 raw chicken carcass and wings
450 g/1 lb leeks, cut into 2.5 cm/1 in lengths
225 g/8 oz no need to soak prunes
Salt and freshly ground pepper

Poach the carcass and wings in water for an hour. Strain, pick the meat from the bones and return the meat to the stock. Add the leeks, prunes and seasoning. Simmer for 30 minutes until the leeks are tender.

Serve with hot oat bread.

Cockie Leekie Soup

EMPANADAS

One of the most famous dishes of all from Argentina, this is a delicious combination of meat and fruit in a little crisp pie. In the original form the pastry is made at home but I strongly recommend you buy the widely available and very excellent puff pastry, as the dish is quite fiddly in its own right. It is however very much worth doing as the pies are unexpected and quite delicious. Serves 4.

INGREDIENTS

1 tbsp oil	1 tbsp fresh chopped parsley
1 small onion, finely chopped	half a pear, peeled and cored
Half a leek, finely chopped	half a peach, peeled and stoned
1 level tbsp plain flour	225 g/8 oz cooked and chopped chicken
150 ml/¼ pint chicken stock	Salt to taste
1 tsp paprika	450 g/1 lb puff pastry
¼ tsp ground cumin	Oil for deep frying (optional)
¼ tsp freshly ground black pepper or chilli powder	

To make the filling, heat the oil in a large pan and gently fry the onion and leek until the onion is translucent. Add the flour, stirring it round until it browns, then add the chicken stock, paprika, cumin, pepper or chilli powder and the parsley. Cook for a minute, stirring so it all blends together.

Chop the pear and the peach and add to the sauce along with the chicken, season to taste. Let the mixture cool before making the empanadas.

Roll out the pastry until you have a sheet about 3 mm/⅛ in thick. You then cut it into circles. The size really depends on how big you want the empanadas to be, but about 13–15 cm/5–6 in across is probably about right. Place a generous amount of the filling in the middle of each circle, then fold over and press the sides together so you have what looks remarkably like a Cornish pasty. Crimp the edges together securely so the filling doesn't seep out while you are cooking them.

You can either deep fry empanadas or bake them in the oven, which obviously uses a lot less fat. To deep fry them, use a large deep pan and fill it with enough oil so the empanadas float while they are cooking. To test when the oil is hot enough, drop in a small piece of bread. If it sizzles the oil is ready. Don't overcrowd the pan and watch them all the time, turning them so they turn golden evenly on both sides. Drain them well on a wire rack. If you prefer to cook them in the oven, put them on a baking tray, allowing space for them to expand, brush with a little beaten egg and cook in a medium oven, 350˚F/180˚C/160˚C Fan/Gas Mark 4/bottom of an Aga roasting oven, for 25–30 minutes until golden. Serve hot as a starter or as a main course with a green salad.

Empanadas

STUFFED TOMATOES

Make this simple dish in the summer and autumn when continental-style 'beef' or Marmande tomatoes are plentiful and cheap. It's quite surprising how delicious and fresh-tasting the tomatoes are, even when cooked. Serves 4.

INGREDIENTS

4 large tomatoes	50 g/2 oz fresh white breadcrumbs
1 clove of garlic, crushed with 1 tsp salt	1–2 spring onions, chopped
15 g/½ oz butter	50 g/2 oz chicken livers, chopped
2 tbsp chopped parsley	

Pre-heat the oven to 400°F/200°C/180°C Fan/Gas Mark 6
Cut the tomatoes in half horizontally and scoop out the pulp, roughly chop and put to one side. Mix together the breadcrumbs, garlic salt and spring onions.

Melt the butter in a pan and fry the livers for 1 minute. Add the breadcrumb mixture and fry for 2 minutes. Add the tomato pulp and fry for 2 minutes. Fill the tomato shells with this mixture and bake for 15 minutes. Sprinkle with the parsley and serve hot.

MINI CHICKEN TIKKA

In an ideal world these can be a hot component of your canapés although they're perfectly delicious eaten cold as well. The only time consuming bit is the threading the bits onto skewers. You can use small bamboo skewers, readily available in supermarkets as well as speciality cook shops, or cocktail sticks work very well if you prefer. Makes 12.

INGREDIENTS

350 g/12 oz boneless chicken breast, skinned	3 tbsp natural yoghurt
2 garlic cloves, crushed or 1 tsp garlic purée	1 tsp ginger purée
Pinch of salt	2 tsp tandoori mix
2 tbsp mango chutney (smooth or with the bits chopped reasonably fine)	Shredded lettuce, to serve

Cut the chicken into 1 cm/½ in cubes. Mix together the yoghurt, garlic, ginger, salt and tandoori mix and stir in the chicken cubes. Leave to marinate for at least 30 minutes or up to 12 hours.

Thread onto bamboo skewers or cocktail sticks, about three cubes to a skewer, and grill for 2–3 minutes on each side. Pack them all together when you do this so that the heat is evenly spread. When they are cooked, i.e. browning but not baked hard, brush with a little mango chutney and serve, either hot or allow to cool and chill for up to two hours. A bed of shredded lettuce is the most attractive way of presenting them.

Mini Chicken Tikka

CHICKEN LIVERS WITH MUSHROOMS AND GRAPES

Chicken livers are combined into a quickly cooked first course with the generously flavoured muscat Italia style grapes and oyster mushrooms, making a starter both earthy and exotic. Serves 4.

INGREDIENTS
225 g/8 oz chicken livers
100 g/4 oz oyster mushrooms
50 g/2 oz Italia white grapes, split and seeded
150 ml/¼ pint water
1 dsp arrowroot or cornflour
50 g/2 oz butter
4 slices of toast

Wash and trim the chicken livers, cutting into pieces about the size of half a walnut. Trim and rinse the oyster mushrooms and cut those into pieces approximately the same size. Stir the arrowroot into the water. You can use cornflour but the sauce will be cloudy.

Melt half the butter in a sauté or deep sided frying pan and sauté the chicken livers until golden on all sides, about 2–3 minutes. Season lightly, add the grapes and the oyster mushrooms and continue to cook over a high heat for another 1½–2 minutes.

Using a large glass or cup as a template, cut rounds from each of the slices of toast, butter the rounds and place each one on a serving dish. Spoon the mushrooms, grapes and chicken livers onto the pieces of toast. Add the water with the arrowroot mixed into it into the pan. Stir round, scraping up all the bits, and bring rapidly to the boil until it is thick and clear. Check for seasoning and pour over the rounds of toast. Serve immediately.

Chicken Livers with Mushrooms & Grapes

LAYERED CHICKEN TERRINE

This terrine would make a spectacular centre piece to a summer buffet or dinner party or even an elaborate picnic. Serves 8–10.

INGREDIENTS

675 g/1½ lb boneless chicken pieces	3 eggs
1 tbsp lemon juice	2 tbsp chopped fresh tarragon
2 tbsp chopped fresh parsley	300 ml/½ pint double cream
30 g/1 oz butter	225 g/8 oz French beans
150 g/6 oz thin baby carrots	1 tbsp green peppercorns in brine

For the sauce:
600 ml/1 pint tomato sugo
2 tbsp chopped fresh herbs, such as basil or chervil
Pinch of sugar
Seasoning

Preheat the oven to 350°F/180°C/170°C Fan/Gas Mark 4/middle of the Aga roasting oven. Grease a 1.75 litre/3 pint terrine or loaf tin with the butter and line the base with a piece of greaseproof paper.

Remove the skin and any sinews from the chicken. Place in a food processor and whizz until finely minced. Add the eggs and pepper and process until evenly mixed. Then add the lemon juice, tarragon and parsley and process slowly adding the cream. Season with salt to taste.

Top and tail the French beans and trim the carrot. Blanch in boiling salted water for 5 minutes. Drain and rinse under cold running water. Carefully stir the green peppercorns into the chicken mixture.

Spoon a third of the chicken mixture into the terrine and spread evenly to cover the base. Lay the French beans on top, leaving a 1 cm/½ in border all the way around. Cover with half the remaining chicken mixture, then arrange the carrots on top, leaving a border as you did with the beans and cover with the remaining chicken levelling it carefully. Cover the terrine with a piece of buttered greaseproof and then cover with foil and place in a roasting tin. Pour in enough boiling water to come halfway up the sides of the terrine and bake for 40–45 minutes or until a skewer inserted into the centre comes out clean.

Meanwhile, make the tomato sauce. Place the tomato sugo in a bowl and stir in the herbs and add a pinch of sugar to taste. Season well and chill until ready to serve. When ready to serve, turn the terrine out on to a plate and wipe with kitchen paper to remove any butter or liquid. Cut into slices and serve with the tomato sauce.

Layered Chicken Terrine

SALMA GUNDY

Salma gundy is an English hors d'oeuvre that dates back to the early 17th century. Conventionally salma gundy was built up into a kind of sugar cone confection based on a big basin in the middle of the table. Each person helps themselves to a segment of the salma gundy as though taking a section from a cake. Serve with a selection of wholemeal and French bread. Serves 4–6.

INGREDIENTS

2 chicken breasts, cooked and skinned	4 sticks of celery, scrubbed
1 cucumber	2 eating apples, cored but not peeled
2 rollmops, finely chopped	4 tbsp parsley, chopped
4 hard-boiled eggs, finely chopped	2 large pickled gherkins, chopped
2 tbsp capers, roughly chopped	1 bunch of watercress, washed

For the dressings:
2 tbsp white wine vinegar
8 tbsp oil, olive or other salad oil
2 tbsp lemon juice
1 tsp salt
1 tsp sugar

Begin by making two dressings, one of them lemon and the other vinegar. Put half the oil, half the salt, all of the sugar and the lemon juice in one pot and shake thoroughly. Place the remaining oil and salt in a second pot with the vinegar, and shake thoroughly.

Cut the chicken breasts into 1 cm/½ in cubes. Cut the celery stalks once lengthwise, and then across into 5 mm/¼ in pieces. Cut the cucumber once lengthwise, scoop out and discard the seeds, and then slice the halves crosswise into 5 mm/¼ in slices. Cut the apples into rings approximately 5 mm/¼ in thick.

On a large oval dish place a soup plate or small basin (upside down) in the middle. Pile the finely chopped rollmops onto the top of it, and surround with a sprinkling of parsley. Pile the chicken cubes around the base of the basin, piling them up as close to it as possible. Place the hard-boiled eggs in a ring around the chicken and garnish with the gherkins. Dip the apple rings in the lemon dressing and arrange around the basin in an attractive pattern between the hard-boiled eggs and the chopped rollmop. Mix the celery with the remaining lemon dressing. Mix the cucumber with the vinegar dressing, and add the capers. Arrange the celery, and the cucumber and capers, around the dish in alternate rings on top of the other ingredients.

Sprinkle the whole with the watercress leaves, filling in any gaps, and making as attractive a pattern as you can.

Salma Gundy

BANG BANG CHICKEN

Each region of China has its own distinctive style of cooking. Those from the most westerly province of China, from Szechwan, have strong, vivid flavours. This cold chicken dish is very simple to make but is extraordinarily good. It's served in China as a first course, but that doesn't stop you cooking it as a main dish! Serves 4.

INGREDIENTS
1 medium-sized chicken
A piece of lemon rind
2 bay leaves
2 cucumbers, washed
1 crisp head of lettuce

For the sauce:
4 tbsp peanut butter
2 tbsp sesame oil
1 tsp each sugar and salt
½ cup water or chicken stock (see method)
1 tsp chilli oil or 1 tsp Tabasco mixed with 1 tbsp cooking oil

Clean and trim the chicken and put it in a large pan with the lemon rind and bay leaves. Pour in just enough water to cover it and poach gently for 45 minutes to an hour. Make sure it is thoroughly cooked. Allow it to cool and keep the liquid which is now very good chicken stock. Skin the chicken and take the meat off the bones. Cut it into 5 mm/¼ in slices across the grain.

Shred the cucumbers with a sharp knife or through a food processor – the pieces should be about the length of 2 or 3 matchsticks. Wash and dry the lettuce and cut that into very fine ribbons. Mix all the sauce ingredients together in a saucepan and heat gently. If you prefer, you can use some of that chicken stock in place of the water. When it comes to the boil, you will find the sauce thickens and becomes smooth and glossy. Take it off the heat and allow to cool a little.

Arrange the lettuce as a bed on a large serving plate, scatter the shredded cucumber over it, and place the chicken on top of that. Dribble a little of the sauce over the chicken and put the rest of the sauce in a bowl so everyone can help themselves. The sauce is pretty fierce, but its nutty flavour is perfect with the salad and chicken.

Bang Bang Chicken

SESAME CHICKEN SALAD

Chicken salads come in many different guises. We often forget that in parts of Asia, particularly in the south-east of Asia, the Chinese rules about never eating raw food don't apply, and salads have a slightly different flavour and texture to those we're used to. This is one that reflects that, with the use of sesame bringing a hint of the exotic to one of our more common ingredients. Serves 6.

INGREDIENTS
6 boned chicken breasts
100 g/4 oz mange-tout peas
30 g/1 oz sesame seeds
½ Chinese leaf or iceberg lettuce, shredded
1 small red pepper, finely sliced
1 small yellow pepper, finely sliced
2 sticks of celery, finely sliced
100 g/4 oz seedless black grapes, halved
100 g/4 oz firm white mushrooms, finely sliced

For the dressing:
5 tbsp sesame oil (roasted)
2 tbsp white wine vinegar
½ tsp dijon mustard
½ tsp sugar
1 small clove of garlic, crushed
A good pinch of salt
Freshly ground pepper

Cook the chicken breasts by poaching in water or stock in a covered pan for 20–25 minutes until thoroughly cooked. Drain and cut into dice. Cook the mange-tout in boiling water for 3 minutes then drain and run under cold water. (This will keep their bright green colour.)

Toast the sesame seeds in a dry frying pan over a moderate heat, shaking the pan until they are pale gold. Arrange the shredded lettuce onto a serving plate. Arrange the fruit and vegetables in an attractive pattern on the lettuce. Pile the chicken in the middle and sprinkle over the sesame seeds.

Whisk the dressing ingredients together and pour over the salad and serve.

Sesame Chicken Salad

BARBECUED CHICKEN WINGS

Chicken wings are very cheap to buy and once properly trimmed are almost as good as drumsticks to eat. They are also a great favourite with children because they're not quite so large and unwieldy. This recipe gives them a Mexican barbecue flavour. You can add more strong spices like the chilli if you're serving them to adults as well. Serves 6–8.

INGREDIENTS

4 tbsp tomato ketchup
1 tsp Worcester or light soy sauce
½ tsp chilli sauce
½ tsp garlic salt
½ tsp light muscovado sugar
Pinch each of chopped fresh or freeze-dried tarragon and thyme
18 chicken wings

Place the tomato ketchup, chilli sauce, worcester or light soy sauce, garlic salt, sugar, tarragon and thyme in a shallow non-metallic dish and mix well. Trim the chicken wings by removing the thin pointy tip leaving just the elbow and mini drumstick. Put into the marinade, mix well to coat and leave for 15 minutes.

Get the barbecue good and hot or heat the grill to hot and line it with foil to both reflect heat and simplify washing up. Shake the chicken wings when you remove them from the marinade and barbecue or grill them on a rack for 6–7 minutes each side. Make sure they're cooked through. You can, when you turn them, dip them back in any remaining marinade to recoat them.

At the end of the cooking time, allow them to stand for just a minute because the coating can be very hot and burn little fingers.

SPICE ISLAND DRUMSTICKS

This is a super crafty recipe using store-cupboard ingredients – except for the chicken. It is great party food, especially to rescue the culinary side of those cooking catastrophes known as barbecues. Serves 6.

INGREDIENTS

12 chicken drumsticks	6 tbsp tomato ketchup
3 tbsp Worcestershire sauce	3 tbsp soy sauce
2 tbsp made mustard (fresh or jar)	2 tbsp oil
2 tsp garlic salt	1 dsp each basil, thyme and tarragon
1 tsp each cinnamon and ginger	

Mix all the sauce ingredients together thoroughly. Coat the drumsticks, marinate for 10 minutes to 12 hours – the longer the better.

Either cook over a barbecue, turning regularly or pre-heat your oven to

Barbecued Chicken Wings

375°F/190°C/180°C Fan/Gas Mark 5. Place the drumsticks on baking trays and bake for 45 minutes or until browned and sizzling. You could also bake them in the oven and transfer them to the barbecue for the last 5 minutes cooking.

JERK CHICKEN

Jerk chicken is a modern development of a process known throughout tropical countries (English speaking ones that is) as a way of preserving meat. It was used on pork and beef as a salting and seasoning process that kept them from going off in the hot weather. Now however 'jerking', particularly in Jamaica and other parts of the Caribbean, has become a flavouring process similar in some ways to the 'blackened' flavourings used in Creole cooking. It's ideal for barbecues and is much nicer to eat than its rather strange name would suggest. Serves 4.

INGREDIENTS
1 large bunch spring onions, about 6
1 tbsp light muscovado sugar
2 tbsp red wine or cider vinegar
1 tsp salt
2 fresh red chilli peppers or 2 tsp chilli purée
2 sprigs or 1 tsp dried thyme
4 boned chicken breasts, skinless, about 150 g/6 oz each
Avocado and tomato salad, to serve

Trim and roughly chop the spring onions and place in a food processor or liquidizer with the sugar, vinegar and salt, and whizz to a purée. Split the chillis; if using fresh, remove their seeds, roughly chop and add them to the food processor. If the thyme is on branches, rub it between your hands over a sheet of kitchen paper and add the leaves to the spring onion mixture. Blend all the ingredients together until the purée is fairly smooth.

Slash each chicken breast twice on the diagonal and place in a non-metallic dish. Smear the jerk mixture all over and leave them to marinate in the fridge for at least 30 minutes. They will not come to any harm for up to 12 hours.

Barbecue 7.5–10 cm/3–4 in from the hot coals for about 10 minutes on each side until golden brown – make sure the chicken is cooked all the way through. Jerk chicken is excellent eaten with an avocado and tomato salad.

Jerk Chicken with Avocado & Tomato Salad

CHICKEN SHASHLIK

This form of cooking chicken on skewers is one of the most popular dishes in Turkey, and goes back to a time when it was supposed to have been a campfire dish of the Turkish soldiers. You can serve this with rice or burghul which is a kind of cracked wheat that cooks like rice. I always find the dish very moreish so you may want to increase my quantities in order to be sure of having enough. Serves 4.

INGREDIENTS
675 g/1½ lb boneless chicken breasts or boneless thighs
4 tbsp olive oil
Juice of 2 lemons
2 cloves of garlic (crushed)
1 tsp oregano
2 green peppers
1 large onion

Cut the chicken into walnut-sized pieces and place in a bowl with the olive oil, lemon juice, crushed garlic and oregano. Leave to marinate for at least an hour, up to 24 is fine.

De-seed the peppers and peel the onion. Slice the peppers into 2.5 cm/1 in squares and slice the onion vertically around each of its sides to create a number of 'square slices'. Thread the chicken onto metal, flat-sided skewers starting with a piece of green pepper, then 2 pieces of chicken, a piece of onion, 2 pieces of chicken, a piece of green pepper, 2 pieces of chicken and a piece of onion. Pack the ingredients fairly close together towards the tip of the skewer and either barbecue or grill under a hot pre-heated grill for 5 minutes a side. You may wish to baste this with some of the marinade as you go along but discard any unused marinade.

Chicken Shashlik

CHICKEN TERRYAKI

This is an easily accessible Japanese dish. In Japan the meat is cooked on a charcoal barbecue but it is easily done under a grill or in a frying pan grill that keeps the food out of the sauce. Serves 4.

INGREDIENTS
4 boneless skinless chicken breasts
150 ml/6 fl oz bought terryaki sauce
For a home-made sauce:
150 ml/6 fl oz light soy sauce
100 ml/4 fl oz sake
100 ml/4 fl oz mirin (Japanese sweet white wine) or apple juice
Juice of half a lemon
2 tbsp sugar
1 tsp salt

If making the sauce, boil all the ingredients until reduced by one-third. Cool. Marinate the chicken breasts for 2–6 hours in the sauce. Set the grill to very hot or stoke up the barbecue.

Brush the chicken breasts with the marinade as they cook so that they have a glistening coating.

GARLIC GRILLED CHICKEN BREASTS WITH CREAM

This is originally a Turkish recipe. An enterprising restaurateur decided to enrich the classic yoghurt marinade with some rather westernised double cream. The result is an exquisite dish that the sultans would thoroughly have approved of. Serves 2.

INGREDIENTS
4 tbsp each double cream and thick natural yoghurt   **Juice of half a lemon**
2 cloves of garlic   **1 tsp salt**
2 chicken breasts (on or off the bone)

Mix the cream, yoghurt and lemon juice together. Crush the garlic with the salt and add to the cream mixture. Score the chicken breasts with a sharp knife diagonally across at 2.5 cm/1 in intervals. Add to the cream mixture and leave to marinate for at least 2 hours and up to 12 hours, turning occasionally.

Barbecue over hot coals or heat the grill to the maximum temperature for at least 10 minutes. Place the chicken breasts in a foil-lined grill pan and grill or barbecue for 8 minutes each side, until the breasts have crisp brown edges, but are still succulent inside.

Serve with rice or hot pitta bread and a salad.

Chicken Terryaki

STIR-FRY CHICKEN WITH PEPPERS AND MANGE-TOUT

This stir-fry recipe is perfect for summer eating – it's quick to prepare, light to eat, and yet has a surprisingly intense flavour. Serves 4.

INGREDIENTS
350 g/12 oz boneless chicken thighs (about 4 large thighs)
1 large Spanish onion
1 each red and green pepper, cored and seeded
1 clove of garlic
1 cm/½ in piece fresh root ginger or ½ tsp ground ginger
1 dsp cornflour
225 ml/8 fl oz water
2 tbsp soy sauce
2 tbsp oil
225 g/8 oz mange-tout, trimmed
Salt and freshly ground black pepper

Cut the chicken into 1 cm/½ in strips across the grain.

Cut the onion in half, then cut each half into 1 cm/½ in ribbons. Slice the peppers into similar sized pieces. Crush the garlic and ginger together into a fairly smooth paste. Blend the cornflour, water and soy sauce together.

Heat the oil in a frying pan or wok until it's just below smoking point. Add the garlic and ginger mixture, stir for 30 seconds and, before it browns or burns, add the chicken pieces. Stir those round for about 2 minutes, until opaque all the way through and just starting to brown on the outside. Transfer to a plate. Add the onions, peppers and mange-tout to the pan and stir cook over high heat for 3–4 minutes, until the vegetables are hot right through but still have a crunch. Return the chicken to the pan and mix together with the vegetables. Season with a little salt and pepper, then add the blended cornflour. Stir and toss for 1 minute – the sauce thickens and goes shiny and smooth.

Serve hot with rice and, if you like, other Chinese dishes.

Stir-Fry Chicken with Peppers & Mange-tout

SOUTHERN FRIED CHICKEN

This is the recipe that reveals Colonel Sanders' secret. Southern-style fried chicken is succulent because of the steam 'pressure' cooking it has towards the end. Contrary to popular belief, it's shallow fried, not deep-fried. Traditionally this would be served with fried bananas, corn fritters and plenty of mashed potatoes. Give 'em a taste of this and they'll all be singing Dixie! Serves 4.

INGREDIENTS
4 chicken quarters or large chicken pieces
3 tbsp flour
1 tbsp ground cinnamon
1 tsp garlic salt
1 egg, beaten
300 ml/½ pint vegetable oil (approximately)
300 ml/½ pint milk

Cut each chicken portion in half and dust with the flour mixed with the cinnamon and garlic salt. Dip each piece in beaten egg and coat again with the flour mixture. Heat about 5 mm/¼ in–1 cm/½ in depth of oil in a wide frying pan and fry the chicken quickly on both sides to seal it, then – and this is the secret of Southern fried chicken – lower the heat and cover the pan. This will make the chicken crisp on the outside and steamed on the inside. Cook for 15 minutes, removing the lid for the last 5 minutes to crisp it up well. Transfer to a serving dish and keep warm.

To make the gravy, pour almost all the oil out of the pan, add the surplus flour mixture and fry for 1 minute. Stir in the milk, bring to the boil and cook for 2–3 minutes. This will make a thick creamy-coloured gravy to serve with the chicken.

Southern Fried Chicken

BISTILLA

This dish comes from the palaces of North Africa and is a very grand dish indeed. It can be made with a variety of different poultry, and pigeon especially reared for the purpose was much favoured in Morocco. I think though that for modern tastes and for ease of achievement, chicken breasts are better. The pastry used is called filo and can be bought in supermarkets and good food stores all over Britain. It's the forerunner of puff pastry and produces a marvellous crisp coating for the unexpected but delicious filling that this super pie contains. It needs to be served really as the high point in a Middle Eastern meal, perhaps after some houmous and vegetable dips eaten with pitta and followed by a fruit salad scented with rose water. Serves 6.

INGREDIENTS

2–2.25 kg/4½–5 lb chicken	1 onion studded with 2 cloves
½ tsp each of allspice, powdered	1 bay leaf
saffron and ginger powder	4 large sprigs of parsley
1 packet filo pastry (approximately 20 sheets)	8 eggs
2 tbsp caster sugar mixed with	150 g/6 oz butter
½ tsp ground cinnamon	50 g/2 oz flaked almonds

1 extra egg, beaten

Pre-heat the oven to 350°F/180°C/170°C Fan/Gas Mark 4.

Put the chicken, the onion, the spices and the parsley into a saucepan and cover with water and bring to the boil. Turn down to a gentle simmer and cook for an hour. Remove the chicken from the stock and allow both to cool. Skin and bone the chicken and cut the meat into walnut sized pieces. Beat a cupful of the cooled stock into the 8 eggs. Add 2 tablespoons of butter to a non-stick pan and scramble the eggs gently until they're nearly set.

Heat a knob of butter in a small frying pan and saute the almonds until they're light gold and set aside. Melt the remaining butter in a clean pan and brush the inside of a roasting pan at least 5 cm/2 in high with it. Lay a sheet or sheets of filo pastry to line it with their ends falling outside. Brush those with butter and continue to build a layer of pastry 4 or 5 sheets thick. Brush the inside with butter and put in half of the egg mixture, spreading it across the bottom. Cover with another layer of filo, 2 sheets thick, buttering each one, and then sprinkle on half the sugar and cinnamon mixture and half the almonds. Put the pieces of chicken on this and cover with the remaining egg mixture and top with 2 more sheets of filo, buttering between each. Fold in the side sheets at this point, sprinkle on the remaining almonds and top with 2 final sheets of filo. Brush these, not with butter, but with the remaining beaten egg.

Bake the pie for 30 minutes then raise the temperature to 400°F/200°C/180°C Fan/Gas Mark 6. Sprinkle with the remaining sugar and cinnamon and return to the oven for 15 to 20 minutes until the pastry is a deep gold colour. It's traditionally cut not in squares but in diamonds, but you may find it easier to remove from the pan in a more conventional style. It's served on its own as a course in a grand meal.

Bistilla

CHICKEN FLORENTINE

This is a marvellous dish for making a little go a deliciously long way. The addition of spinach and beautiful baked cheese sauce stretches a small amount of chicken into a substantial meal for four. Use fresh spinach if you can – the prewashed packs of spinach you can get in most supermarkets make this very quick to prepare. Serves 4.

INGREDIENTS
4 boned chicken breasts or boneless thighs
300 ml/½ pint water
1 bay leaf
1 small peeled onion
Salt
450 g/1 lb fresh spinach or 225 g/½ lb frozen leaf spinach
30g/1 oz butter
½ tsp grated nutmeg
100 g/4 oz Gruyère or Cheddar cheese

For the white sauce:
300 ml/½ pint milk
30 g/1 oz butter
30 g/1 oz flour

Pre-heat the oven to 375°F/190°C/180°C Fan/Gas Mark 5.
Put the chicken in a saucepan with the water, bay leaf, onion and a little salt. Bring to the boil and immediately turn down the heat and simmer very gently for about 20 minutes.

Rinse the spinach and plunge it into boiling water for a couple of minutes, drain well, then melt the butter and toss the spinach in it. Lay the spinach in an oven-proof dish. When the chicken is cooked, cut it into nuggets and put on top of the spinach.

Make the sauce in a non-stick pan. Whisk together the milk, butter and flour over a medium heat, add a pinch of salt. Just whisk the sauce 3 or 4 times as it is coming to the boil until it is thick and glossy. Mix 75 g/3 oz of the cheese and the nutmeg into the white sauce and pour over the chicken. Sprinkle with the rest of the cheese and bake for 15 minutes until golden and bubbling. It's particularly nice with mashed potatoes.

Chicken Florentine

CHICKEN VERONIQUE

The grapes give a clear sweetness to this classic dish, which is very quick and easy to cook. Muscat grapes are available in summer, and have easily the best flavour, otherwise use seedless green grapes – don't use red grapes in this recipe. Serve simply with pasta or rice. Serves 4.

INGREDIENTS
4 chicken breasts
½ onion stuck with 2 cloves
2 bay leaves
2 fresh parsley stalks
300 ml/½ pint unsweetened white grape juice
2 tsp cornflour (or arrowroot)
150 ml/¼ pint single cream
Juice of half a lemon
150 g/6 oz muscat grapes, halved and de-seeded, or use seedless white grapes
Salt and freshly ground black pepper

Place the chicken breasts in a casserole or saucepan with the onions and herbs and cover with the grape juice. Put the lid on and either simmer or bake in a pre-heated oven 350°F/180°C/170°C Fan/Gas Mark 4 for 20–25 minutes until the chicken is thoroughly cooked.

Remove the onion and herbs and throw them away. Place the chicken breasts on a warm serving dish. Mix the cornflour or arrowroot into the cream and lemon juice then whisk into the cooking liquid in the pan over a medium heat until you have a thick, smooth sauce. Add the grapes and just heat them through for 1–2 minutes, no more, then pour the sauce over the chicken breasts. Check for seasoning and pile the warm grapes around the chicken.

Chicken Veronique

CHICKEN WITH SAUTÉD APPLE SLICES

Chicken, apples and cream are a classic tradition from both sides of the Channel, in Normandy and in Kent. This is a modern style adaptation of those rather more substantial casserole style dishes as it doesn't use a cream sauce. It still however benefits from the ability of chicken to carry a variety of flavours and to benefit from the slightly sweet and sour combination that the apples give it. Mashed potatoes and courgettes go particularly nicely with this. Serves 4.

INGREDIENTS
25 ml/1 fl oz cooking oil (not olive)
4 chicken breasts
100 g/4 oz shallots (or small onions)
1 tbsp cider vinegar
225 ml/8 fl oz freshly pressed apple juice
1 tbsp fresh or 1 tsp freeze-dried tarragon
2 English eating apples
50 g/2 oz butter
1 dsp arrowroot

Sauté the chicken breasts in the oil until they are golden on both sides. Peel and very finely chop the shallots or onion and add that and cook for another 2–3 minutes. Season generously and pour on the cider vinegar. Allow to bubble almost dry and then add the apple juice. Turn the heat to low, add the tarragon, cover the pan and allow to simmer for 20 minutes until the chicken breasts are done right through.

Meanwhile core but don't peel the apples and divide into 12 sections per apple. An apple cutting device is ideal for doing this effortlessly. In a separate pan heat the butter till it foams, add the apples and, over a medium heat, turn until they're golden but not breaking up. To serve, remove the chicken pieces to a serving dish and stir a tablespoon or two of water into the arrowroot and add to the sauce. Stir over a medium heat until the sauce thickens and clears – this will take about 2 minutes. Arrange the apple slices around the chicken and pour the sauce over or under depending on whether you prefer old fashioned or nouvelle presentation.

Chicken with Sautéd Apple Slices

POLLO ROSSO

This is an Italian-style dish in the modern manner, cooked with the fashionable flavours of balsamic vinegar and sun-dried tomatoes. Serves 4.

INGREDIENTS
4 x 150 g/6 oz boned chicken breasts, skinned
1 tbsp olive oil
2 tbsp balsamic vinegar
1 clove garlic, crushed
4 sprig rosemary
2 tbsp sun-dried tomato paste or condimento (a gourmet sauce for pasta)
Salt and pepper

Sauté the chicken breasts in the olive oil for 2–3 minutes a side until lightly golden. Carefully pour in the vinegar and stir all the crusty bits into the liquid. Add the garlic, rosemary and tomato paste or condimento. Turn the chicken to coat it well and add a cup of water, simmer for 15 minutes or until the chicken is cooked through, spooning the sauce over it occasionally and turning it once. Season to taste – it may not need anything. Serve with rice or noodles.

SUPREME OF CHICKEN WITH ASPARAGUS

The French have a name for a boneless piece of chicken cut from the breast. They call it the supreme, and I think that, teamed with asparagus, this is really chicken with class! If you want to use fresh asparagus – cook it first for about 10 minutes until still a little crisp and use the top 12.5 cm/5 in. Serves 4.

INGREDIENTS
1 tbsp vegetable oil
30 g/1 oz butter
4 breasts of chicken, boned
125 ml/5 fl oz water
1 tbsp flour
125 ml/5 fl oz double cream
225 g/8 oz packet frozen asparagus, thawed (or a can will do)
½ tsp salt
Freshly ground black pepper

Heat the oil and butter together in a large pan and fry the chicken for 5 minutes. Add the water, cover and cook gently for about 15 minutes. Remove the chicken and keep warm on a serving dish.

Whisk the flour into the liquid, then whisk in the cream. Add the asparagus, reserving a little for garnish, season to taste and heat through until boiling. Pour over the chicken and garnish with the reserved asparagus to serve.

Pollo Rosso

COUNTRY CAPTAIN

Country Captain is an extraordinary name for a dish that was developed in India by the Anglo-Indian community during the Raj, particularly in regimental messes where it was the favourite Sunday lunch dish. I think of it as a chicken curry that is eaten best with the curry accompaniments – poppadoms, plenty of rice, chutney and perhaps a cucumber raita – grated cucumber and spring onions mixed into a bowl of thick yoghurt. Serves 4.

INGREDIENT S
450 g/1 lb onions
1 garlic clove
2 tbsp sunflower oil
1 tbsp mild curry powder or curry paste
1 medium to large (1.5 kg–2 kg/3–4½ lb) chicken, or eight chicken pieces
400 g/14 oz can coconut milk or 225 g/8 oz coconut cream mixed with
300 ml/½ pint boiling water
225 g/8 oz frozen peas
1 tbsp lemon juice
1 tbsp light muscovado sugar
Poppadoms, plain boiled rice, chutney and cucumber raita, to serve

Peel and thinly slice the onion and the garlic and fry in the oil over a medium heat until golden brown. Add the curry powder or paste and stir thoroughly and fry for another 2 minutes. Add 225 ml/8 fl oz of water, bring to the boil and allow the water to evaporate until the onions and spices are frying again and fragrant.

Cut the chicken into 8 pieces, if using a whole chicken, and add to the pan, turning thoroughly in the flavoured onion and oil mixture. Add the coconut milk or coconut cream mixture, stir to mix and simmer for 20–30 minutes or until the chicken is cooked through. Add the frozen peas, the lemon juice and sugar. Stir, bring to the boil and leave to stand for a couple of minutes before serving with poppadoms, rice, chutney and raita.

Country Captain

CHICKEN POLO

Chicken Polo is a subtle and delicately spiced Persian dish. Basmati rice is the best one to use, but any good long-grained rice will do. If you are serving this for a dinner party use chicken breasts, otherwise you can make it with very cheap chicken pieces like legs or thighs. All the spices, cinnamon, cardamom and saffron, are easily available in supermarkets. Serves 4.

INGREDIENT S
25 ml/1 fl oz olive oil
30 g/1 oz butter
1 clove garlic, finely chopped
275 g/10 oz basmati or long-grain rice
2 bay leaves
1 stick of cinnamon
2 pods cardamom
4 chicken pieces
600 ml/1 pint chicken stock (homemade or stock cube)
A pinch of saffron (optional)
Salt
A few chopped almonds

In a large solid frying pan heat the oil and then the butter in that order – the butter cooks in the oil and does not burn. Add the garlic and fry until pale gold – don't let it burn. Add the rice, turning it until it is translucent. Put in the bay leaves, cinnamon and cardamom pods and then add the chicken. Fry the rice and chicken together for about 5 minutes until the chicken is pale gold, then add the stock. The trick of good rice is to have exactly double the quantity of liquid to rice by volume, that way the rice absorbs exactly the right amount of liquid. Add the saffron if you are using it, and a good pinch of salt. Stir the whole thing and let it cook very gently for about 20 minutes with a cover on.

The chicken cooks through in the stock. Its flavours get absorbed by the rice and the saffron turns it gold, while the garlic, bay leaves, cinnamon and cardamom flavour and scent it like a spice market. For the last 5 minutes take the lid off to make sure all the liquid is absorbed. Serve it on a large platter with almonds sprinkled over it.

Chicken Polo

THAI CHICKEN CURRY

Unless you have a very good supermarket near to you, you may need to go to a speciality shop to obtain fresh ingredients for a Thai curry. If you can't get fresh herbs and ginger try dry ones. A little anchovy essence can be used instead of shrimp paste. Serves 4.

INGREDIENTS
1 tbsp ground coriander
1 tbsp finely chopped garlic
1 tbsp finely chopped galingale, also known in Thailand and Malaysia as
Laos or Thai ginger
½ tbsp each ground red chilli and paprika
1 tsp each salt, grated lime peel and ground black pepper
1 small onion
1 stalk of lemon grass
4 tbsp oil
225 g/8 oz coconut cream (I think it's easiest to buy this in tins which are
very readily available)
300 ml/½ pint hot water
1 tsp shrimp paste
450 g/1 lb chicken breast, boned
225 g/8 oz button mushrooms
30 g/1 oz chopped green coriander leaf

Put the ground coriander, garlic, laos, chilli, paprika, salt, lime peel, black pepper, the small onion peeled and rough chopped, the lemon grass cut into 1 cm/½ in pieces and half the oil, into a blender and process till a smooth paste (you could do this by hand with a mortar and pestle).

Put the coconut cream into a large saucepan and bring it to the boil. Add the spice mixture and cook over a low heat for about 10 minutes until the spices give off their aroma. Cut the chicken into pieces the size of half a walnut, add to the coconut milk and spices and cook for 7–8 minutes until cooked through. Add the button mushrooms, halved if they are largish, and the shrimp paste. Stir and simmer for 3–4 minutes. Sprinkle with the chopped coriander and serve with rice.

Thai Chicken Curry

THE CRAFTY ROAST CHICKEN

This is my favourite chicken recipe of all time – it's also the one most favoured by my family. It's a very simple way of roasting a chicken, a task that may seem to need no instruction, but this technique produces a delicately flavoured bird that's moist and delicious, with a crisp skin and succulent flesh, whether it's eaten hot with a cream sauce or cold with salad. It can also be used for chicken portions – simply reduce the cooking time. This recipe follows an early crafty tradition of using garlic salt. While I use it a great deal less than I used to, on this occasion it's quite the best and simplest way of achieving the flavour. Serves 4–6.

INGREDIENTS
1 x 1.5–1.75 kg/3–4 lb roasting chicken
1 tsp each garlic salt, powdered bay leaves and paprika

| Half a lemon | Freshly ground black pepper |
| 2 tbsp cream | 1 dsp cornflour |

Pre-heat your oven to 375°F/190°C/180°C Fan/Gas Mark 5.
Make sure the chicken is at room temperature. Remove all the giblets and any surplus fat from the cavity. Squeeze the lemon over the whole chicken, then place the squeezed half inside the cavity.

Sprinkle the garlic salt, bay leaves and paprika over the top, sides and legs of the chicken, putting a small pinch inside the cavity on each occasion, and season with pepper to taste.

Place in a baking dish into which it just fits comfortably. Cover with 1 or 2 used butter papers (with some butter still sticking to them) or lightly butter a piece of foil and lay it over the top of the chicken. The intention is not to wrap the chicken in the paper or foil, but merely to keep it moist and basted with butter during its cooking. Roast for about 45 minutes. Remove the paper or foil for the last 15 minutes – it will have browned pretty thoroughly underneath it anyway. Allow the chicken to stand for 5 minutes after you take it out of the oven to reabsorb its juices. The total cooking time should be, depending on the size of the chicken, about 1 hour to 1½ hours. Check for doneness by pushing a skewer into the thigh – if the juices aren't clear cook another 15–20 minutes and repeat the test.

If you want to eat it just as it is, carve it, remove the surplus fat from the juices in the dish and use for gravy. If you prefer a fancier method of serving, cut into joints and place on a serving dish. Heat the juices in the pan with 2 tablespoons of cream mixed with 1 dessertspoon of cornflour and about half a cup of water. This will produce a wonderful herby, garlicky cream sauce to pour over the chicken. If you want to eat it cold, allow it to cool under the butter papers, in the pan it was cooked in before putting it in the fridge. You will find that it will remain moist and flavoursome for 24 hours without needing to be wrapped in foil or clingfilm. It's particularly nice in the summer, cut into portions and served with a salad that includes some fruit, particularly white grapes.

The Crafty Roast Chicken

POUSSIN STUFFED WITH KUMQUATS AND PINE NUTS

Poussin are the small size chickens that are available everywhere now. They're actually fully mature chickens grown specially for their size and have a considerable though delicate flavour. They are also quite substantial and a whole one stuffed is probably more than a person can eat on their own, especially if the meal has more than one or two courses. I find that half a poussin cooked in this way per person makes a wonderful main course in a dinner that has a starter and a dessert to go with it. I think this is particularly nice served with some green beans or mange-tout peas. Serves 4.

INGREDIENTS
2 large or 4 individual poussin, oven-ready
100 g/4 oz long grain or basmati rice
30 g/1 oz each olive oil
30 g/1 oz butter
50 g/2 oz pine nuts
30 g/1 oz orange marmalade
8 kumquats (tiny baby oranges the size of the first joint of your thumb)
1 bunch of spring onion, green and white parts finely chopped
Pinch of nutmeg
Salt and pepper
225 ml/8 fl oz fresh orange juice (optional)

Pre-heat the oven to 400°F/200°C/190°C Fan/Gas Mark 6/middle of the roasting oven in the Aga. Put the rice to boil in a pint of salted water. When it's barely cooked, about 8–9 minutes, drain it thoroughly.

Melt the butter in the oil and fry the pine nuts in it gently for about 2–3 minutes until they are gold. Add the marmalade and allow that to melt. Add the drained rice and the spring onions. Add the nutmeg and season generously with salt and pepper and mix thoroughly together off the heat.

Cut the kumquats into quarters, remove any seeds that emerge, and mix with the rice. Stuff the poussin carefully with the rice, putting any extra stuffing into a baking dish. Season the poussin and roast them, with the surplus stuffing alongside, for 50 minutes. Check if the chickens are done by putting a skewer or sharp knife into the thigh. If they show any pink juices allow them to cook for another 10 minutes and check again.

To serve: if you have used large poussin split them in half lengthwise with a big sharp knife and pile the stuffing onto the warm plate and cover with the half poussin, skin side up. Serve individual poussin whole.

You can, if you wish, make a little sauce to go with the chicken by adding 225 ml/8 fl oz of fresh orange juice to the pan they were roasted in, bringing it to the boil, stirring all the bits in, and providing that in a jug to pour over the poussin and rice.

Poussin Stuffed with Kumquats & Pine Nuts

CHICKEN PROVENÇALE

A rich and sunny chicken casserole that can be cooked on top of the stove as well as in the oven. Olives, anchovies, tomatoes and herbs combine to make the famous French provençale flavour. It's often served with wide, flat noodles to take up the sauce, although rice is nice with it too. If you can't find any passata, liquidized or sieved tinned tomatoes are an alternative. Serves 4.

INGREDIENTS
2 tbsp olive oil
6 chicken joints (2 breast, 2 thighs, 2 drumsticks)
1 onion, chopped
1 red pepper, chopped
1 clove of garlic, crushed
450 ml/18 fl oz passata
1 tsp dried basil and oregano (mixed)
Salt and freshly ground black pepper
4 anchovy fillets
6 black olives

Heat the oil in a deep frying pan with a lid and fry the chicken pieces until brown on both sides. Add the onion, pepper, garlic, passata and herbs and season to taste. Stir and cook for about 25 minutes until the chicken is tender and cooked through. Dot the olives and anchovy fillets on top and serve with plenty of flat noodles.

RIVIERA CHICKEN

Full of the warmth and colours of the sun, this way of cooking a chicken is a meal in a dish. All you need is a salad and some fruit to complete the Riviera dream. Serves 4.

INGREDIENTS
1 x 1.75 kg/4 lb chicken	2 cloves of garlic, peeled
1 lemon	2 tbsp oil

450 g/1 lb new potatoes, scrubbed
450 g/1 lb cherry tomatoes
1 tsp basil
1 tbsp chopped parsley

Pre-heat the oven to 350°F/180°C/170°C Fan/Gas Mark 4.
In an ovenproof pan or casserole, brown the chicken in the oil for 3 minutes. Chop the garlic and add it, squeeze the lemon over and bake covered for 30 minutes. Cut the potatoes into 1 cm/½ in dice, add and continue to bake for 25 more minutes. Then add the tomatoes and dried basil and heat the tomatoes through. Sprinkle with the parsley, carve (or section with scissors) and serve.

Chicken Provençale

PAELLA

Paella, the most famous of Spanish dishes, is a fabulous celebratory meal. It is rice-based with an adventurous combination of meat, fish and vegetables cooked in one large open pan. Serves 6.

INGREDIENTS
6 chicken portions
4 tbsp olive oil
2 cloves garlic, peeled and chopped
1 large bunch spring onions, finely chopped
350 g/12 oz basmati or patna rice
½ tsp saffron
½ tsp each fresh chopped or freeze-dried rosemary and thyme
100 g/4 oz carrots, cubed
100 g/4 oz peas
100 g/4 oz stringless green beans, cut into 1.5 cm/½ in pieces
1.2 litres/2 pints fresh scrubbed and cleaned mussels
225 g/8 oz large prawns, preferably unpeeled and raw
Salt and freshly ground black pepper

In a large frying pan, at least 2.5 cm/1 in deep, heat the oil and fry the chicken pieces until golden. Add the chopped garlic and spring onions. Measure the rice by volume in a jug, then pour it into the pan. Stir for 2–3 minutes until the rice is glistening. Using the same jug to measure, add twice as much water by volume as of rice. Stir in the saffron and herbs and simmer for 25 minutes.

Add the vegetables, and stir. Check that all the mussels are closed (throw away any that are not) and place them on top of the rice with the prawns. Cover loosely and steam over a medium to low heat for 5–7 minutes until the prawns are pink and the mussels have opened. This time check to make sure that all the mussels have opened and throw away any that have not.

Stir the mixture gently, season and serve the paella, if possible, in the pan in which it was cooked.

Paella

KYOTO NOODLE BOWL

Noodles are to Japan what almost all other kinds of fast food are to the rest of the world. There are noodles bars where we would find a hamburger joint. There are noodle bars where we would expect to find a café. The food that is served in them is always served in individual portions but the portions are very large, as a bowl of soup noodles is an alternative to a full meal. The ingredients vary and can range from very simple, totally vegetarian dishes with just bean curd and one or two vegetable flavourings to complex arrangements which include fish and meat. This is a simple but, I think, delicious mixture which I first tasted at the noodle bar in the railway station of Japan's ancient capital, Kyoto. Serves 4.

INGREDIENTS
350 g/12 oz Udon noodles or thick spaghetti
1 large raw chicken breast, boned and skinned
2 carrots
4 spring onions
2 mushrooms
1.2 litres/2 pints fresh chicken stock
2 tbsp of soy sauce
225 g/8 oz fresh spinach
4 eggs

In a large saucepan put 1.75 litres/3 pints of water, bring it to the boil, add a pinch of salt, and the noodles. Boil for 3 minutes, cover and leave to stand for 7 more minutes and then drain.

Slice the chicken breast very thinly across the grain, peel and slice the carrots very thinly across the grain, top and tail the spring onions and cut into 5 mm/¼ in rounds. Trim the mushrooms, and wash carefully, criss-cross the top like a noughts and crosses board with a sharp knife.

To cook: put a cup of the stock into a saucepan with half the soy sauce. Add the carrots, bring to the boil and simmer for 5 minutes. Add the chicken slices and the spring onions and simmer 5 minutes more. Cut the spinach into 1 cm/½ in ribbons, place in pan with the remaining chicken stock and bring to the boil. Add the chicken and carrot mixture, and the mushrooms, and simmer 2 minutes.

Divide the noodles into 4 large individual soup bowls and ladle the vegetable and chicken mixture onto them, making sure that everybody gets an even sharing of the mushrooms, chicken and vegetables, and topping up afterwards with the soup, which should be at boiling point. Break an egg into each bowl and cover with a plate and leave for 3 minutes for the egg to set before serving.

Kyoto Noodle Bowl

COUS COUS WITH CHICKEN AND TOMATOES

Cous cous is the fine cracked wheat that when steamed swells up like rice. In its original form it takes quite a long time to cook, but almost all the cous cous you buy in Britain these days (and it's extremely widely available not only in health food stores but also supermarkets), is already pre-cooked and therefore takes no more than 20–30 minutes. The sauces or stews that go with the cous cous are as varied as there are cooks in North Africa, but in Algeria they particularly favour sauces coloured and tasting of tomatoes, and are also fond of chicken rather than lamb as the main meat. Serves 4.

INGREDIENTS
1 chicken, cut into portions
4 tbsp olive oil
2 cloves of garlic, chopped
1 medium onion, sliced
1 tbsp tomato purée
100 g/4 oz cooked chick peas (tinned are easiest)
2 carrots, cut into batons
4 large ripe tomatoes, each cut into 8 pieces
30 g/1 oz chopped parsley
350 g/12 oz cous cous
Salt and pepper

Fry the chicken pieces in half the olive oil until lightly browned. Add the onion and garlic, the tomato purée and enough water just to cover the chicken. Season generously and simmer for 10 minutes. Then add the cooked chick peas, the carrots and the tomatoes.

Mix the cous cous with its own volume of water, seasoning and the remaining olive oil. Stir it and leave it to swell up for about 15 minutes. To cook: place it in a colander or sieve over a pan of boiling water (traditionally it's done over the stew but this can be hazardous), steam for 20–25 minutes until swollen and cooked through.

To serve: stir a knob of butter into the cous cous and pile in a ring around a large dish. Spoon the chicken and vegetables into the centre of the dish and pour the sauce over separately. It can have a little chilli sauce added to give it extra pungency.

Cous Cous with Chicken & Tomatoes

INDEX